Frib

Get **more** out of libraries

Please return or renew this item by the last date shown.
You can renew online at www.hants.gov.uk/library
Or by phoning 0845 603 5631

Hampshire
County Council

D0411818

SHAKESPEARE RETOLD

A MIDSUMMER NIGHT'S DREAM

by

Martin Waddell & Alan Marks

W
FRANKLIN WATTS
LONDON•SYDNEY

First published in 2009
by Franklin Watts
338 Euston Road
London NW1 3BH

Franklin Watts Australia
45–51 Huntley Street
Alexandria
NSW 2015

Text copyright © Martin Waddell 2009
Illustrations copyright © Alan Marks 2009

Editor: Jackie Hamley
Designer: Peter Scoulding
Series Advisor: Dr Catherine Alexander of the
Shakespeare Institute, University of Birmingham

A CIP catalogue record for this book is available
from the British Library.

ISBN: 978 0 7496 7743 5 (hbk)
ISBN: 978 0 7496 7749 7 (pbk)

Printed in China

Franklin Watts is a division of
Hachette Children's Books,
an Hachette UK company.
www.hachette.co.uk

CONTENTS

THE CAST

The Nobles of Athens
Duke Theseus – ruler of Athens
Queen Hippolyta – his bride-to-be
Hermia – in love with Lysander
Lysander – in love with Hermia
Demetrius – in love with Hermia
Helena – Hermia's friend, in love with Demetrius
Hermia's father – wants Hermia to wed Demetrius

The Fairies
Oberon – king of the fairies
Titania – queen of the fairies
Puck – a sprite, Oberon's servant
Fairies – Peasblossom, Cobweb, Moth and Mustardseed

The Workmen of Athens
Bottom – a weaver
Peter Quince – a carpenter
Flute – a bellows-mender
Snout and Snug – other workmen

PROLOGUE

A fairy king quarrels with his fairy queen
in an enchanted wood where confused lovers
meet, kiss, cry and kiss again.
A playful spirit's tricks confuse as a weaver
wears an ass's head and plain men plan a play.

Is it real, or all a wondrous dream ...

... dreamt on a midsummer night?

CHAPTER ONE

LOVE LOSES

Duke Theseus of Athens had won a war,
but lost his heart to the queen he'd
taken prisoner. Capturing a queen
is no way to make her love you,
but this time it had worked.
Theseus wanted to show
everyone that love had
triumphed over a
bad beginning with a
lavish wedding to
Queen Hippolyta.

"Time to celebrate!"
the happy duke
exclaimed.

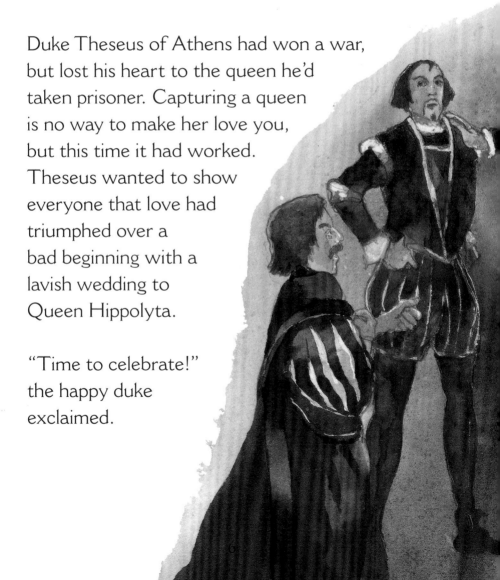

Then in came an angry nobleman, a girl in tears, and two quarrelling young men who loved her.

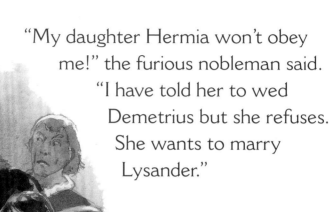

"My daughter Hermia won't obey me!" the furious nobleman said. "I have told her to wed Demetrius but she refuses. She wants to marry Lysander."

"You know the law of Athens!" the duke told Hermia. "If you disobey your father and refuse to wed Demetrius, you die!"

"But I love Lysander!" Hermia sobbed.

"And I love Hermia," Lysander told the duke. "I am as good as Demetrius. Why shouldn't I marry Hermia?"

Duke Theseus had to uphold Athenian law, whether or not the young couple were in love. "Wed Demetrius or die!" he told Hermia sternly.

"The course of true love never did run smooth!" Lysander told Hermia when at last they were alone. "We'll run away together. Meet me in the wood tomorrow!"

And Hermia agreed.

This should have been all right, but Hermia told her best friend Helena of the plan.

"I must do it! I don't love Demetrius! I'd die before I'd marry him!" she said.

"And I'm dying for love of Demetrius!" Helena sighed. "I love him but he never looks twice at me."

Then, as if things weren't muddled enough, Helena, desperately hoping to win favour with Demetrius, told him what Hermia and Lysander were planning.

"I'll go to the wood after them!" Demetrius swore. "I'll fight Lysander if I have to!"

Helena decided she would follow Demetrius, hoping that somehow she might win his love. Hope is all some lovers have and, sometimes, hope wins.

CHAPTER TWO

ENTER BOTTOM THE STAR!

As the moon rose that midsummer night, four young lovers were heading for the wood. Four young lovers, and Bottom the weaver and his friends.

Bottom wasn't in love with anyone but himself. He and his friends had come to the wood to rehearse a play they were going to present at the duke's wedding celebration.

BOTTOM THE WEAVER
in Peter Quince's
The MOST TRAGICAL
COMEDY AND MOST CRUEL
DEATH OF PYRAMUS
AND THISBE

with additional dialogue by
BOTTOM THE WEAVER
Stage Managed by
BOTTOM THE WEAVER
Directed by Peter Quince assisted
by BOTTOM THE WEAVER
Settings suggested by
BOTTOM THE WEAVER
Printed and published by
BOTTOM THE WEAVER

11

"You play Pyramus the lover!" Quince the carpenter told Bottom. "He kills himself for love at the end."

"I'll make everyone weep!" Bottom said. "Mind you, I could be frightening as well."

Then Bottom bounced about being frightening. Everyone was frightened.

"Flute!" said Quince. "You play Thisbe, the girl Pyramus loves!"

"A girl?" gasped Flute the bellows-mender.

"I could play Thisbe!" Bottom suggested.

He wisped and lisped about being a woman who looked just a bit like a rather fat weaver. Everyone cheered.

"Snout!" said Quince. "You play the lion."

"I would be a good lion!" Bottom boasted,
and he roared like a lion. Everyone jumped.

"Duke Theseus might hang us all if
your roaring scared the ladies,"
Quince pointed out.
Everyone was horrified.

"I'll roar you like a
nightingale!" Bottom
said, and he did.
Everyone was relieved.

"You can't play all the
parts!" Peter Quince
insisted, so Bottom
agreed to be Pyramus.

Everyone knew Bottom
would be brilliant
because he was
BOTTOM THE STAR!

CHAPTER THREE

LOVE HURTS

Others were out in the wood, not the play-actors
or the young lovers. Others that they couldn't see,
a fairy king and his queen, ill-met by moonlight.
They were quarrelling like the lovers at court.

The argument was about one of their servants.
Queen Titania flounced off in a furious sparkle,
followed by the fairies who served her.

The angry King Oberon summoned Puck,
the most mischievous of all the spirits.

"I'll teach my proud Queen Titania a lesson!"
he told Puck, ordering the sprite to fetch a
flower called love-in-idleness.

"I'll squeeze the juice of the flower on Titania's
eyelids as she sleeps," Oberon laughed. "When
she wakes, she'll fall in love with the first thing
she sees! A lion, a wolf, a bull? A monkey would
be good, or an ape! When she does what I want,
I'll undo the spell!"

"I'll fly round the world till I find it!" Puck said, and he disappeared to do Oberon's bidding.

At that moment, along came the angry Demetrius looking for Hermia and Lysander, followed by the lovesick Helena. Neither of the humans could see or hear Oberon, for he was a spirit, but he could see and hear them.

"Don't follow me!"
Demetrius swore.
"You know I've come
to save Hermia from
Lysander. I don't love
you. Go away!"

Helena wouldn't go.

"I get sick when I look at you!" Demetrius said
cruelly. "I'll run off and hide, leaving you here at
the mercy of the beasts!"

"I can't fight for love as men
do," Helena said sadly. "But
I'll follow you just the same."

The invisible Oberon
was horrified by the
way Demetrius had
spoken to the poor girl.
He decided to do
something about it.

"I'll turn things round before you leave this wood!" Oberon swore. But they couldn't hear him.

When Puck returned, Oberon put the love potion on Titania's eyes. He ordered the sprite to cast the same enchantment on the young Athenian the fairy king had seen in the wood.

And that's where it all went wrong!

CHAPTER FOUR

LOVE CONFUSES

Tired and confused, the young lovers became lost and separated in the wood. Lysander, Demetrius and Hermia all fell asleep exhausted, while Helena was still searching for Demetrius.

Oberon had ordered Puck to enchant the young Athenian he had seen in the wood, but Puck found the wrong Athenian.

He laid the love potion on the eyelids of the sleeping Lysander, not Demetrius.

When Oberon realised what the sprite had done, he put the love potion on Demetrius' eyelids himself, so that both young men were enchanted.

"Bring Helena here! When Demetrius wakes, he will see her and fall in love," Oberon commanded Puck.

"Lord, what fools these mortals be!" sighed Puck when he returned with Helena.

Then Lysander woke up before Demetrius and saw Helena. "I love you forever, Helena!" Lysander cried.

"Don't make fun of me!" Helena said bitterly.

Their arguing woke Demetrius, and the first person he saw was Helena.

"Helena, you goddess! I love you," he cried, falling instantly in love with her just as Oberon had planned.

"But you said you loved Hermia," Lysander objected angrily. "You can have Hermia now. I don't want her!"

"And I don't
want her either!"
Demetrius swore.
"How could I love
Hermia when sweet
Helena is here?"

Their angry voices woke
Hermia and she heard
every word. "Nobody
loves me!" Hermia gasped.
"Everybody loves Helena!"

But Helena didn't believe any of them.
"I hate you all!" she said angrily.

"Why hate me, Helena?" Hermia asked.

"Because you're all in it together!
You're all teasing me!" Helena sobbed.

Then Helena ran off weeping, and
the young men ran after her.

Hermia followed in despair.

The mischievous Puck led them astray by imitating their voices, so they all got lost in the dark wood.

When they fell asleep, Puck seized his chance and put the love potion on Lysander's eyes, making sure the young man saw Hermia when he woke.

Everyone had the right lover at last!

Then Puck made more mischief ...

CHAPTER FIVE

BOTTOM THE ASS!

The sprite found Bottom and his friends rehearsing their play in another part of the wood. What the actors didn't know, and Puck did, was that Titania was sleeping close by.

Puck's mind whirled, remembering Oberon's plan. Suppose when the enchanted Titania awoke, the first thing she saw was Bottom the weaver? And what if she saw a *changed* Bottom? Puck purred and Puck danced and Puck grinned with delight, and then set his magic to work.

One minute Bottom was Bottom the weaver ...
the next he was Bottom the ass!

It was too much for Quince and the other actors!
They fled through the dark wood.

Puck darted through the trees, appearing to them
as a horse, then a headless bear, then a hound,
then a fire blazing round them. His neighing and
grunting and roaring and burning scared the
actors out of their wits.

Bottom didn't understand why his friends had run away screaming. He didn't know he had huge ears and looked like an ass with a human body. He thought the others were playing a trick to frighten him.

"They'll not make an ass out of me!" Bottom swore. And he stayed where he was, singing quietly to himself to show everyone just how scared he *wasn't*, as people do, when they are really scared.

Bottom's singing woke the sleeping Titania.
She opened her eyes and saw …
Bottom the ass!
Of course she fell in love at once.

"Sing to me! Sing your beautiful song to me again,
oh my love!" gasped the enchanted Titania.

It wasn't every day, or every midsummer night,
that Bottom found himself embraced by
a beautiful fairy queen in an enchanted wood.

The queen's fairy servants, Peasblossom, Cobweb, Moth and Mustardseed, fluttered round him. They fed Bottom purple grapes, green figs and mulberries and honey.

Bottom fell asleep in the arms of the queen.

32

If he heard
laughter, it
was the laughter
of Oberon and the
mischievous Puck,
as they watched the
queen woo an ass.

Bottom started to snore and Oberon came forward, seizing his chance to win his argument with the queen.

"About our servant …?" he began.

"Do what you want! I'm too busy being in love with this gorgeous creature!" cooed Titania.

Then Oberon removed the enchantment.

"How could I be in love with that?" gasped Titania.

"No matter, sweet queen!" laughed Oberon.

Their argument forgotten, the fairy king and queen smiled at each other once more.

In a flash, Puck undid his spell, and
Bottom was Bottom again!

When Bottom woke up he thought he had
dreamed the best dream that ever a weaver
dreamed. He rushed off to tell his friends
about it.

CHAPTER SIX

LOVE CONQUERS

As morning dawned, Duke Theseus came to the wood with his huntsmen. He was surprised and pleased to find that everything had been sorted out between the young lovers, though quite how that had happened the duke didn't know.

Demetrius, still enchanted, told the duke that he
loved Helena and could never marry Hermia.
That meant that Lysander, released from his
enchantment with Helena, could marry Hermia,
the girl he really loved.

"We'll celebrate all three weddings together!"
the duke told the lovers, and Hermia's father
had to agree.

"I'm afraid we've got Quince the carpenter's
play to watch first!" someone sighed.

"What play is that?" asked the duke.

"The Most Awful Play Ever!" the same
someone replied, and everyone groaned.

"Oh well, if we must," laughed the duke,
leading them all back to the palace.

Quince the carpenter brought his actors on to the stage. And the play? The play was so bad that the audience loved it. They'd never seen anything like it before, especially the weaver in the starring role.

Bottom
strutted.

Bottom
cried.

Bottom died,
several times,
and ...

... the audience cheered!

Then the actors and audience joined in the
Wedding Dance, all happy together.

When everyone had left and the night was still, the duke's hall suddenly filled with sweet music. Titania and Oberon danced with the spirits, and they sparkled and glowed and sang their blessing to the lovers. No one saw them come and no one saw them go. They went softly, leaving the lovers to love.

EPILOGUE

A fairy king, a fairy queen,
four lovers, a playful spirit, plain men
and a weaver with an ass's head.
It seemed they'd shared a wondrous dream …

… dreamt on a midsummer night.

NOTES

by Dr Catherine Alexander

A Midsummer Night's Dream opens with plans for a grand wedding between Theseus, Duke of Athens, and Hippolyta, Queen of the Amazons. It has often been thought that when Shakespeare wrote the play (in the mid 1590s) it was for the entertainment at a real aristocratic wedding. This may even have been attended by Queen Elizabeth.

The play is frequently performed and many think that it is Shakespeare's funniest. But like many of his comedies, it begins seriously with the threat to Hermia's life. Then it works towards the traditional happy ending of multiple marriages.

The play is funny, romantic and magical. Shakespeare cleverly combines different strands of plot: the story of the four young lovers; the story of Oberon, Titania and the fairies; and the story of Bottom and his friends performing their play.

These strands come together, are muddled and then unravelled in the wood outside Athens. 'Wood' has a number of meanings. It is obviously a place with trees but it is also a pun. In the play, Demetrius says, 'And here am I, and wood within this wood'. By this, he means that he is 'wooed' by Helena who is pursuing and courting him. This could also mean that he is, in an Elizabethan sense of the word, going mad.

Many characters explain their adventures in the wood as dreams – they assume they must have been asleep – and the title of the play invites the audience and readers to think of the story as a dream as well.

A Midsummer Night's Dream finishes with an epilogue – a special speech in which one of the characters speaks directly to the audience and encourages them to appreciate what they have seen. In the play, it is delivered by Puck.
He playfully encourages the watchers to think they have been sleeping and dreaming too.

If we shadows have offended,
Think but this, and all is mended:
That you have but slumbered here,
While these visions did appear;
And this weak and idle theme,
No more yielding than a dream.

A MIDSUMMER NIGHT'S DREAM FACTS

❖   As the wood is such a strange place where characters dream and unusual things happen to them it has been presented in many different ways on stage.

❖   Charles Kean's production in 1858 had 54 fairies in its wood and Ellen Terry, who was only eight years old and would become a very great actress, playing Puck. She rose through a trap door in the stage, sitting on a mushroom.

❖   Frank Benson's production of 1889 had 24 girls and 16 boys dancing in the wood.

❖   The play has frequently been performed in the open air to take advantage of natural features. Beerbohm Tree tried to create a realistic wood in 1900 and included real rabbits on stage.

❖   In 1970 Peter Brook famously set the whole play in a white box. Oberon and Puck watched the action in the wood from above while hanging from trapezes.

❖   The magic of the play has inspired many artists and musicians. One of the first English operas, Henry Purcell's *The Fairy Queen* of 1692, is loosely based on the play, and Benjamin Britten's *A Midsummer Night's Dream* opera of 1960 cleverly used singers to represent the trees in the wood.